Barn Quilt Trails Around America
Coloring Book
John H. Lettau

Featuring Barn Quilt Patterns Located in...

Shawano County Wisconsin
Green County Wisconsin
Gibson County Indiana
Franklin County Vermont
Lake County California
Delaware County Iowa
Tennessee Appalachian Trails
Flint Hills Kansas Trails
Central & Northwestern Kansas Trails

History of Barn Quilts

 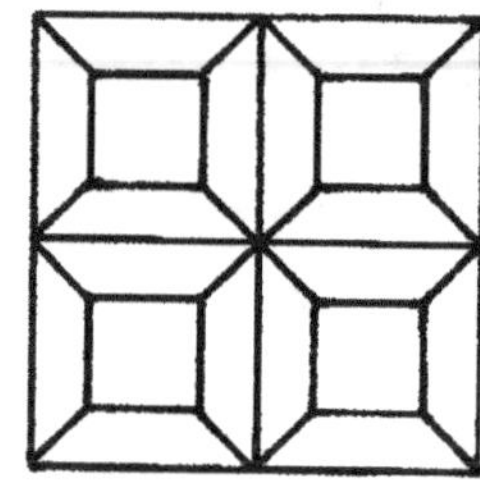   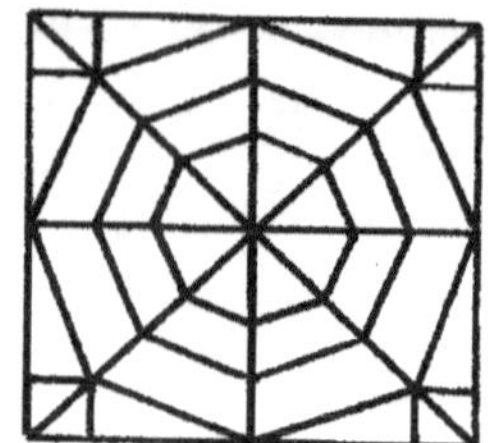

Today colorful barn quilts,"quilt blocks," can be found along many highways, rural back roads and even in towns and cities through-out America and Canada. The interest in this fast growing grass root arts movement started not many years ago in Ohio and continues to grow daily as communities, social groups and clubs see what barn quilts can do to promote tourism and the local history/heritage. Brilliant barn quilt patterns are displayed on barns, corn cribs, and other farm out-buildings through out farm country and even in towns and cities. Five examples barn quilt patterns in this book are pictured above… Mariner's Compass, Spools, Peruvian Horse, Folded Star and Homecoming. This book is an opportunity for you to create many original color design patterns for the above patterns.

Barn Quilt Projects are usually supported and organized to educate, promote and celebrate the unique agricultural heritage of an area through the visual combination of barns and quilt patterns, Farms are vital to the economic well-being of many rural communities. Handmade quilts provided warmth, beauty, and an outlet for individual artistic expression. Plus, tourism is an important part of local barn quilt projects.

Information on How Barn Quilts are Constructed

A barn quilt is made by painting a barn quilt design on two 4' by 8'sheets of 3/4 inch plywood suitable for weathering out door in all forms of weather. Prior to painting the barn quilt pattern two or three coats of primer are applied to front, back and all edges of the plywood. Next, draw the barn quilt pattern. Frog Tape (painter tape) is then applied to outline all section of the design. Two coats of each color are painted, with each coat allowed to dry overnight. After the quilt is finished it is allowed to dry and cure for two weeks before being mounted on a barn or other building.

Each quilt design is usually painted by a team of volunteers and require a willing farmer owner to donate hanging on their barn or other structure. Making these quilt squares allows volunteer groups from churches, schools, 4-H, other community service groups, and even families the opportunity to create and paint their own quilt square as a group project. The chosen square may represent a family pattern from a beloved family quilt.

Interesting Facts on Barn Quilts

1. Common designs, such as Corn & Beans, are found in many states & rural areas.
2. The same quilt pattern will be found with different color patterns.
3. It is not uncommon to find the same pattern with different names.
4. Some common patterns have small modifications with a few extra lines.
5. Barn quilt patterns may honor individuals, families, and/or groups.
6. Many times color selections may have a special family meaning.
7. Quilts maybe family designed and named.
8. Some city libraries and social clubs are organizing senior coloring programs.
9. Some select a common pattern and just change coloring pattern.and/or name.
10. Some find popular patterns and change the name with a new meaning.

Typical Barn Quilt Project Objectives

1. Reflects the agricultural heritage of the region.
2. Barns or buildings are highly visible from highway or road.
3. Have building bring pride to the area.
4. Protes well maintained barns and other farm buildings.
5. Promotes tourism for and in the area.

Objectives of Coloring Books

1. Provide a relaxing for seniors and families.
2. Reduce tension & tension in daily life.
3. Create a fun activity for all age groups.

Delaware County Iowa Barn Quilts

Double T   Four Tulips   9rh Infantry Division
Homecoming   Summer Blooms   Yankee Puzzle
Prairie Queen   North Star   Iowa Sun

Green County Wisconsin Barn Quilts

Cornucopia   Centennial   Kayak
Blazing Star   Farmer's Daughter   Little Giant
Constellation   North Star   Four Stars

Lake County California Barn Quilts

Monkey Wrench   Three Cheers   Courthouse Steps
Blazing Sun   Hawaiian Pineapple   Grape Expectations
Flowers and Ferns   Olive Wreath
Oak Leaf   Double Wedding Ring   Checkered Rooster
Celtic Knot   Tess in the Garden

Gibson County Indiana Barn Quilts

Wild Stag   Mariner's Compass   Home of the Kickapoos
Chicken Scratch   Fleur-de-lis   Drunken Path
Hunter's Star   Summer Dayz   Potted Flower
Compass Star   Double Wedding Ring
Posie Whirl   Fleur-de-lis

Flint Hills Kansas Barn Quilts

Straight & Narrow   Egg Basket   Which Way North
Tennessee Compass   Farm Star   State Fair Sunflower
Rising Star   Rock Cross   Delectable Star

Franklin County Vermont Barn Quilts

Star Explosion   Bicycle Wheel   Tulips in Bloom
Dove Inside Heart   Stars & Lilies   Chained Star Variation
Windblown Lily   Friendship

Appalachian Trail Tennessee Barn Quilts

Tennessee Tulip   Tri-Color   Flower Basket
Stained Glass Star   Eye of God   Purple Tulips & Gold
Cordian Knot   Chicago Star   Snow Crystals
County Fair   Jubilee Star   Diamond Knot

Shawano County Wisconsin Barn Quilts

Wayne's Dilemma   Autumn Leaves
Optical Illusion   Peruvian Horse   Liberty Banner
The Red Rooster   Gamma Ray Burst   Barn Raising   Whirlygig
Star Bound   Star of Empire   Wintry Reflection   Twisted Star
Farmer's Pride   Snowy Morning   54-50 or Fight
Sara's Star   Wisconsin   Castor & Pollux

Central & Northwestern Kansas Barn Quilts

Nancy's Fan   Mexican Tile   Christmas Cactus
Mariner's Compass   Interlocking Blocks   Spools   American Legion
Folded Star   Scully the Golden Retriever   Stars & Bars
4H Star   Patriotic Star

Barn Quilt Double **T** Delaware County Iowa

Barn Quilt Four Tulips Delaware County Iowa

Barn Quilt 9th Infantry Division Delaware County Iowa

Barn Quilt Homecoming Delaware County Iowa

Barn Quilt Summer Blooms Delaware County Iowa

Barn Quilt Yankee Puzzle Delaware County Iowa

Barn Quilt Prairie Queen Delaware County Iowa

Barn Quilt North Star Delaware County Iowa

Barn Quilt Iowa Sun Delaware County Iowa

Barn Quilt Cornucopia Green County Wisconsin

Barn Quilt Centennial Green County Wisconsin

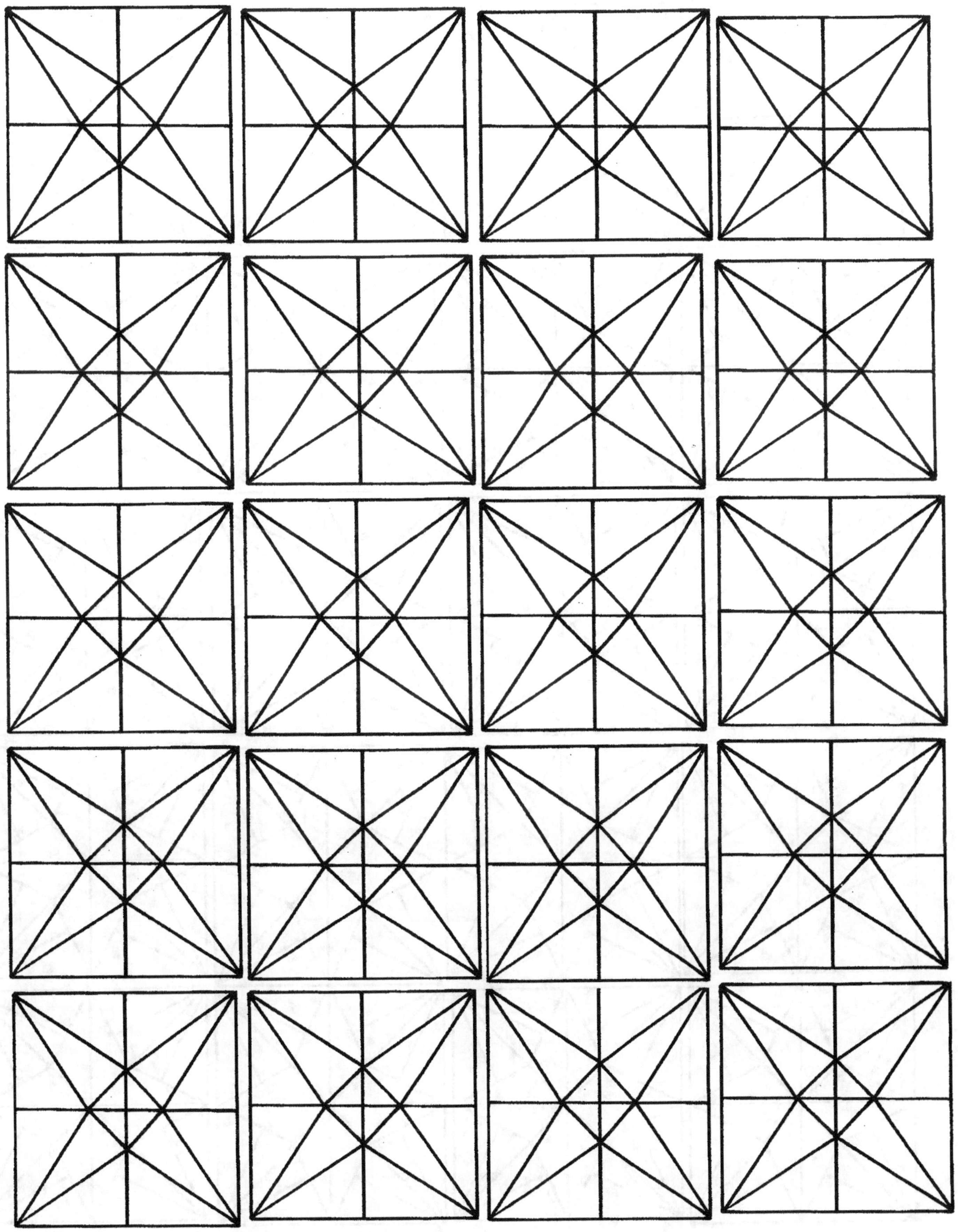

Barn Quilt Blazing Star Green County Wisconsin

Barn Quilt Farmer's Daughter Green County Wisconsin

Barn Quilt Little Giant Green County Wisconsin

Barn Quilt Constellation Green County Wisconsin

Barn Quilt North Star Green County Wisconsin

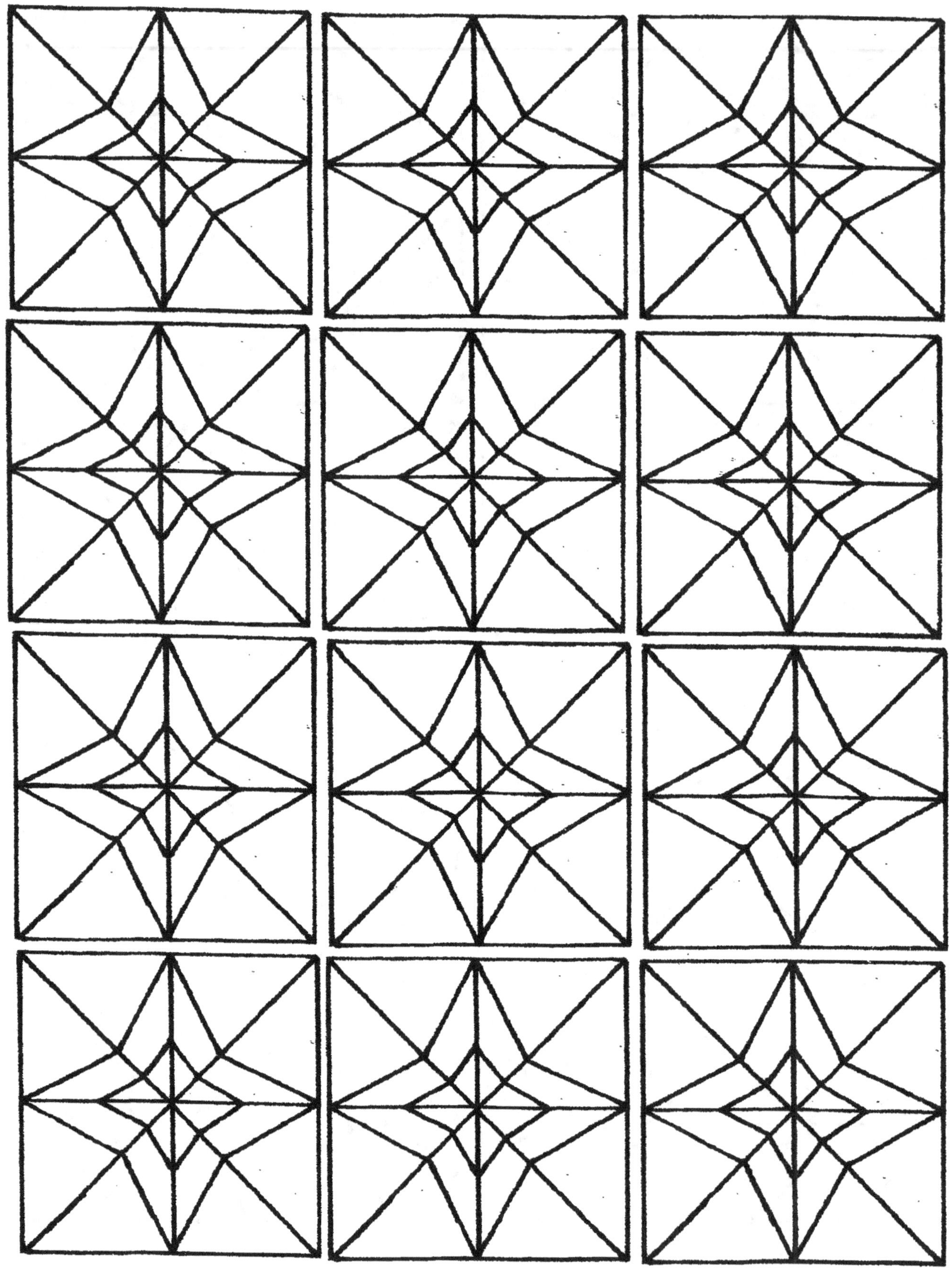

Barn Quilt Four Stars Green County Wisconsin

Barn Quilt Monkey Wrench Lake County California

Barn Quilt Three Cheers Lake County California

Barn Quilt Courthouse Steps Lake County California

Barn Quilt Blazing Sun Lake County California

Barn Quilt Hawaiian Lake County California

Barn Quilt Grape Expectations Lake County California

Barn Quilt Flowers & Ferns Lake County California

Barn Quilt Olive Wreath Lake County California

Barn Quilt Oak Leaf Lake County California

Barn Quilt Double Wedding Ring Lake County California

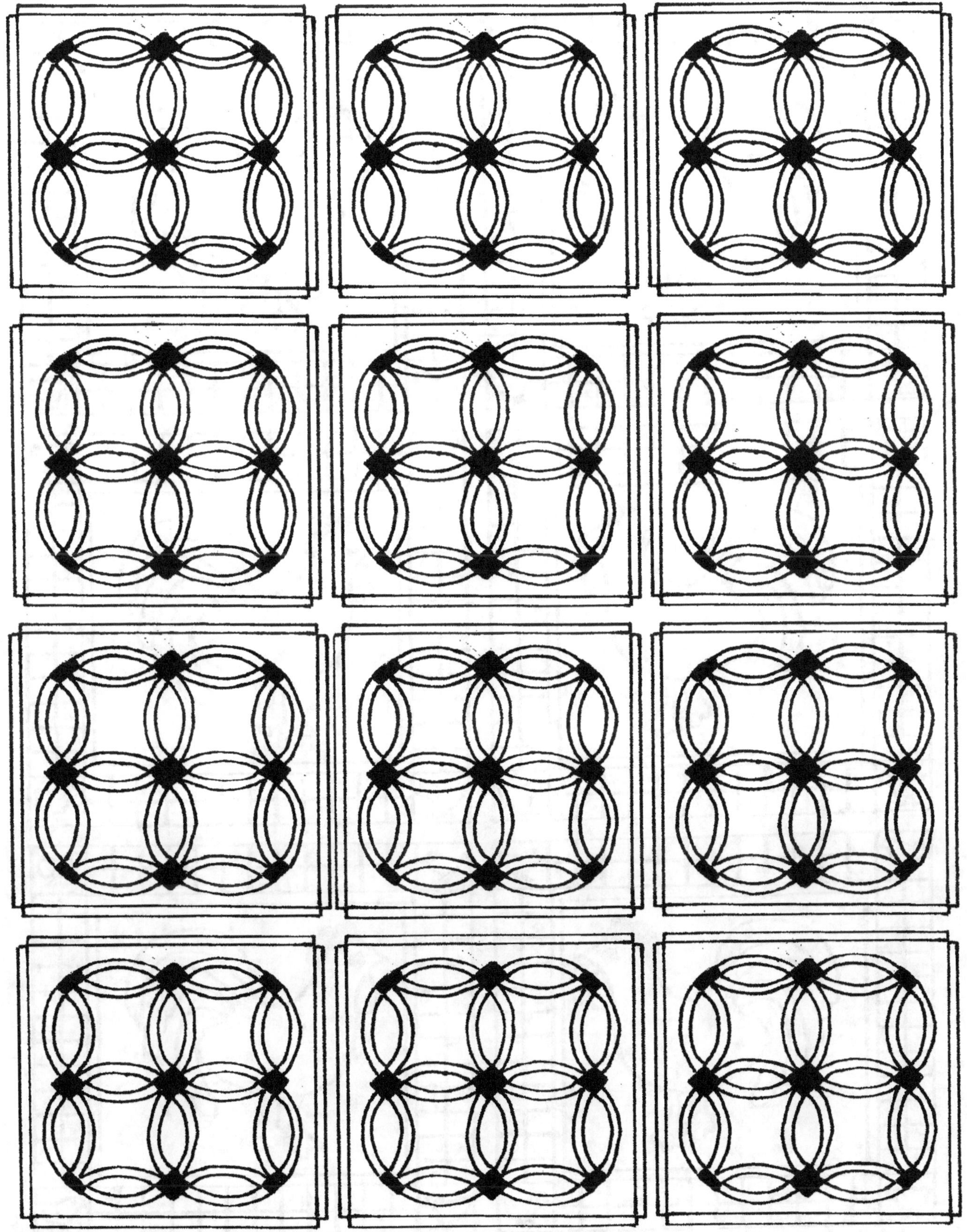

Barn Quilt Checkered Rooster Lake County California

Barn Quilt Celtic Knot Lake County California

Barn Quilt Tess in the Garden Lake County California

Barn Quilt Wild Stag Gibson County Indiana

Barn Quilt Mariner's Compass Lake County California

Barn Quilt Home of the Kickapoos Gibson County Indiana

Barn Quilt Chicken Scratch Gibson County Indiana

Barn Quilt Fleur-de-lis Gibson County Indiana

Barn Quilt Drunken Path Gibson County Indiana

Barn Quilt Hunter's Star Gibson County Indiana

Barn Quilt Summer Dayz Gibson County Indiana

Barn Quilt Potted Flowers Gibson County Indiana

Barn Quilt Double Wedding Ring Gibson County Indiana

Barn Quilt Posie Whirl Gibson County Indiana

Barn Quilt Fleur-de-lis Gibson County Indiana

Barn Quilt Straight & Narrow Flint Hills Kansas

Barn Quilt Egg Basket Flint Hills Kansas

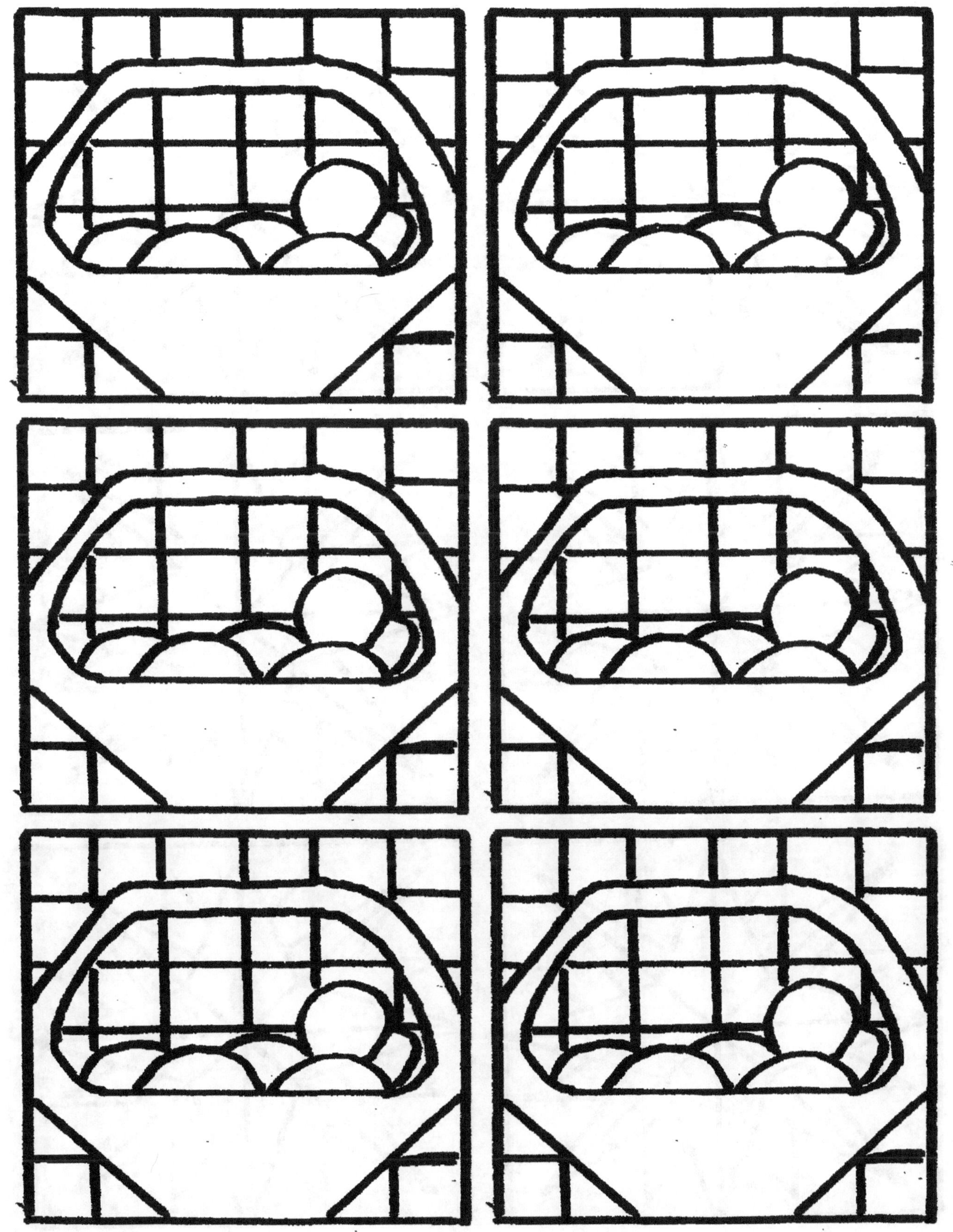

Barn Quilt Which Way North Flint Hills Kansas

Barn Quilt Tennessee Compass Flint Hills Kansas

Barn Quilt Farm Star Flint Hills Kansas

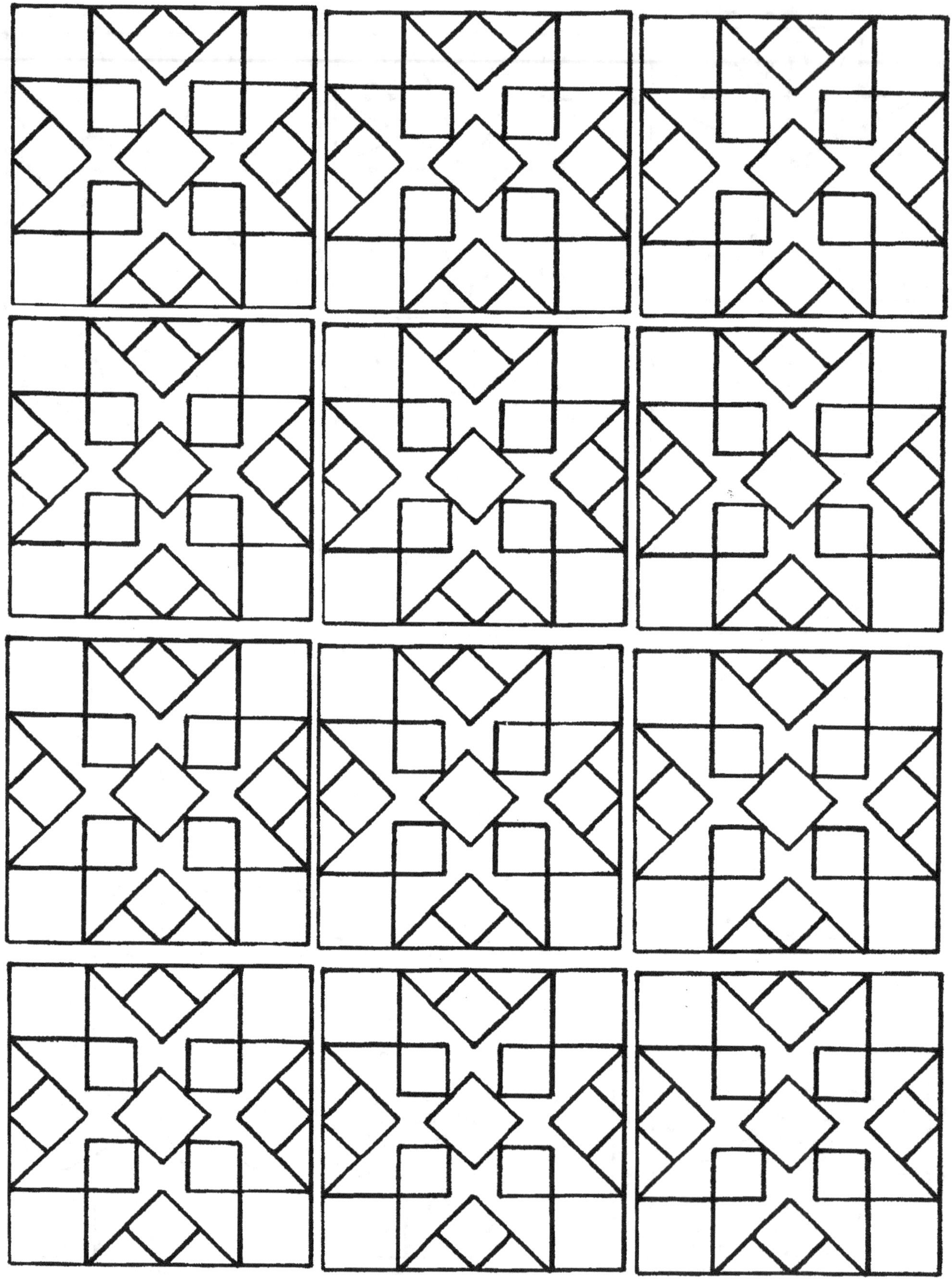

Barn Quilt State Fair Sunflower Flint Hills Kanasa

Barn Quilt Rising Star Flint Hills Kansas

Barn Quilt Rock Cross Flint Hills Kansas

Barn Quilt Delectable Stars Flint Hills Kansas

Barn Quilt Star Explosion Franklin County Vermont

Barn Quilt Bicycle Wheel Franklin County Vermont

Barn Quilt Tulips in Bloom Franklin County Vermont

Barn Quilt Dove Inside Heart Franklin County Vermont

Barn Quilt Star & Lilies Franklin County Vermont

Barn Quilt Chained Star Variation Franklin County Vermont

Barn Quilt Windblown Lily Franklin County Vermont

Barn Quilt Friendship Franklin County Vermont

Barn Quilt Tennessee Tulip Appalachian Trail Tennessee

Barn Quilt Tri-Color Star Appalachian Trail Tennessee

Barn Quilt Flower Basket Appalachian Trail Tennessee

Barn Quilt Stained Glass Star Appalachian Trail Tennessee

Barn Quilt Eye of God Appalachian Trail Tennessee

Barn Quilt Purple Tulips & Gold Appalachian Trail Tennessee

Barn Quilt Gordian Knot Appalachian Trail Tennessee

Barn Quilt Chicago Star Appalachian Trail Tennessee

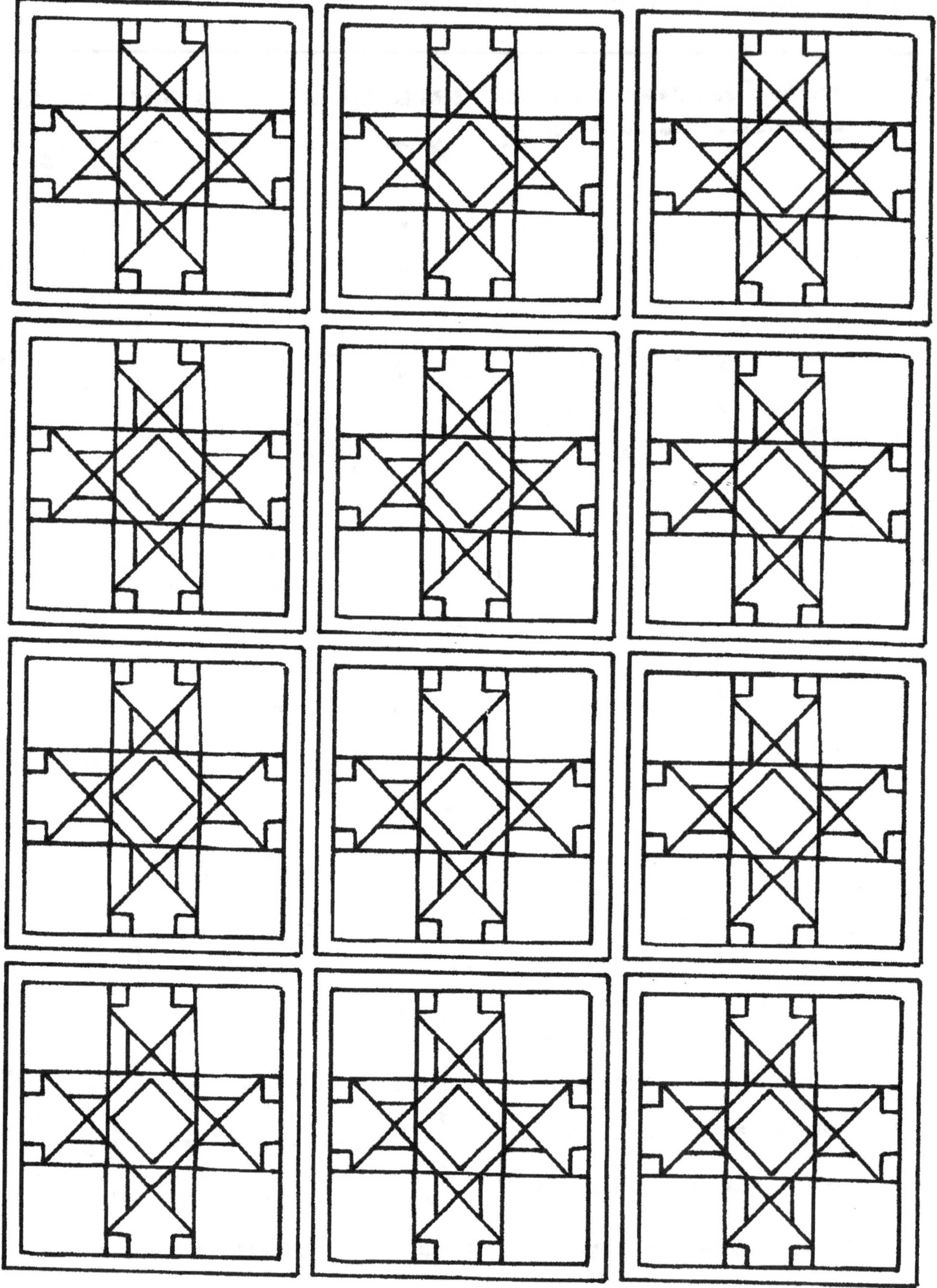

Barn Quilt Snow Crystals Appalachian Trail Tennessee

Barn Quilt County Fair Appalachian Trail Tennessee

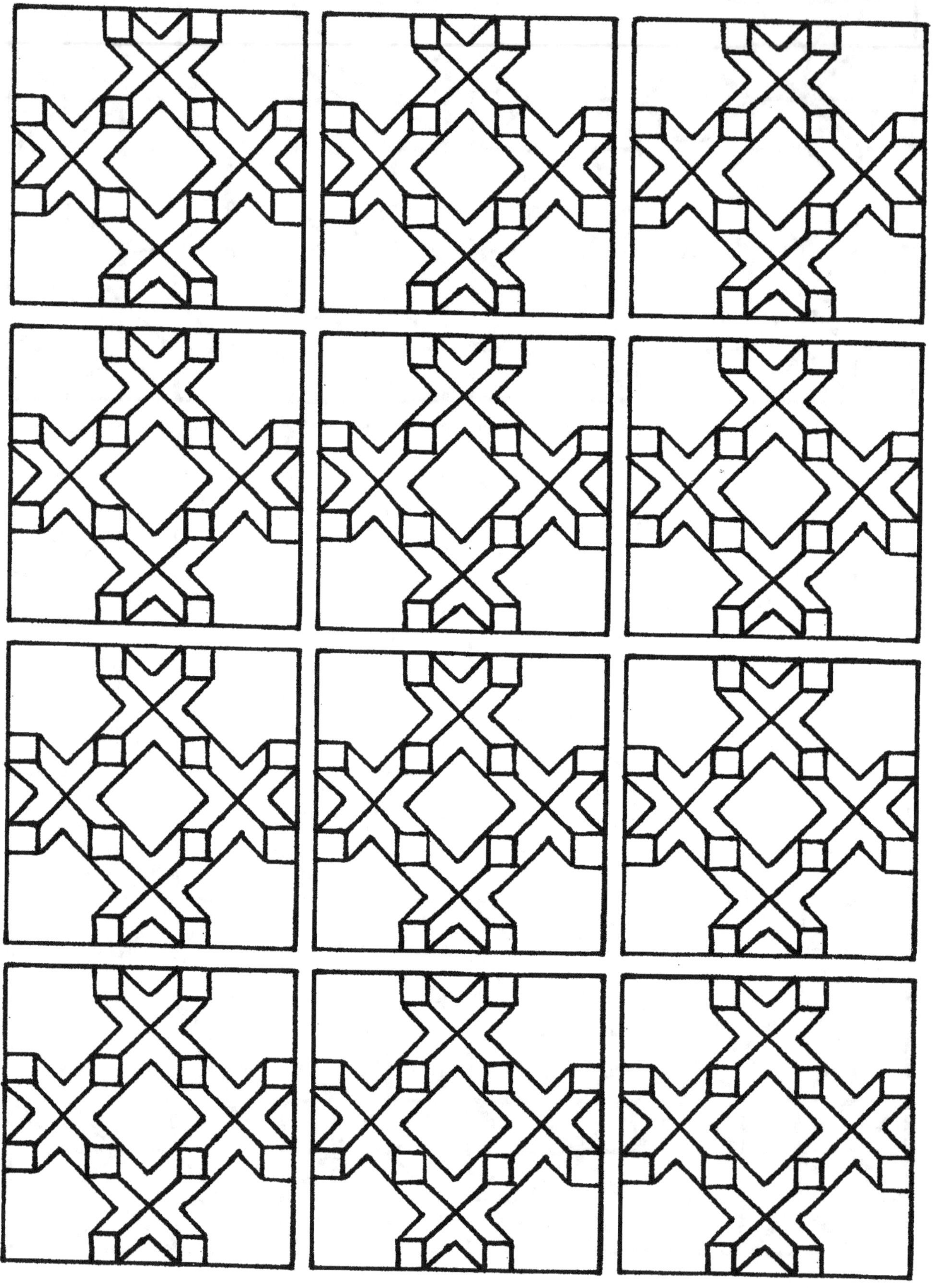

Barn Quilt Jubilee Star Appalachian Trail Tennessee

Barn Quilt Diamond Knot Appa;achian Trail Tennessee

Barn Quilt Wayne's Dilemma Shawano County Wiisconsin

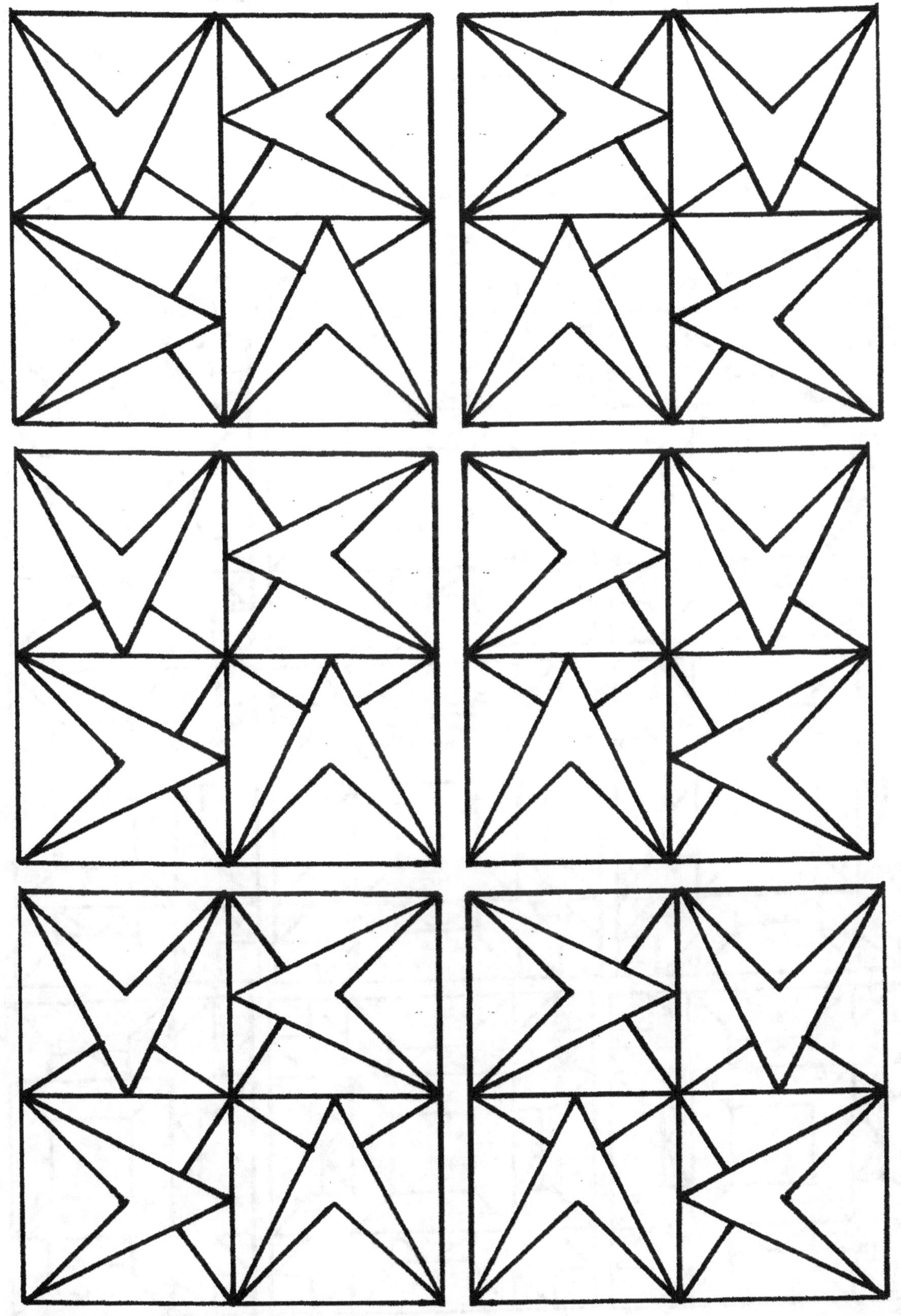

Barn Quilt Autumn Leaves Shawano County Wisconsin

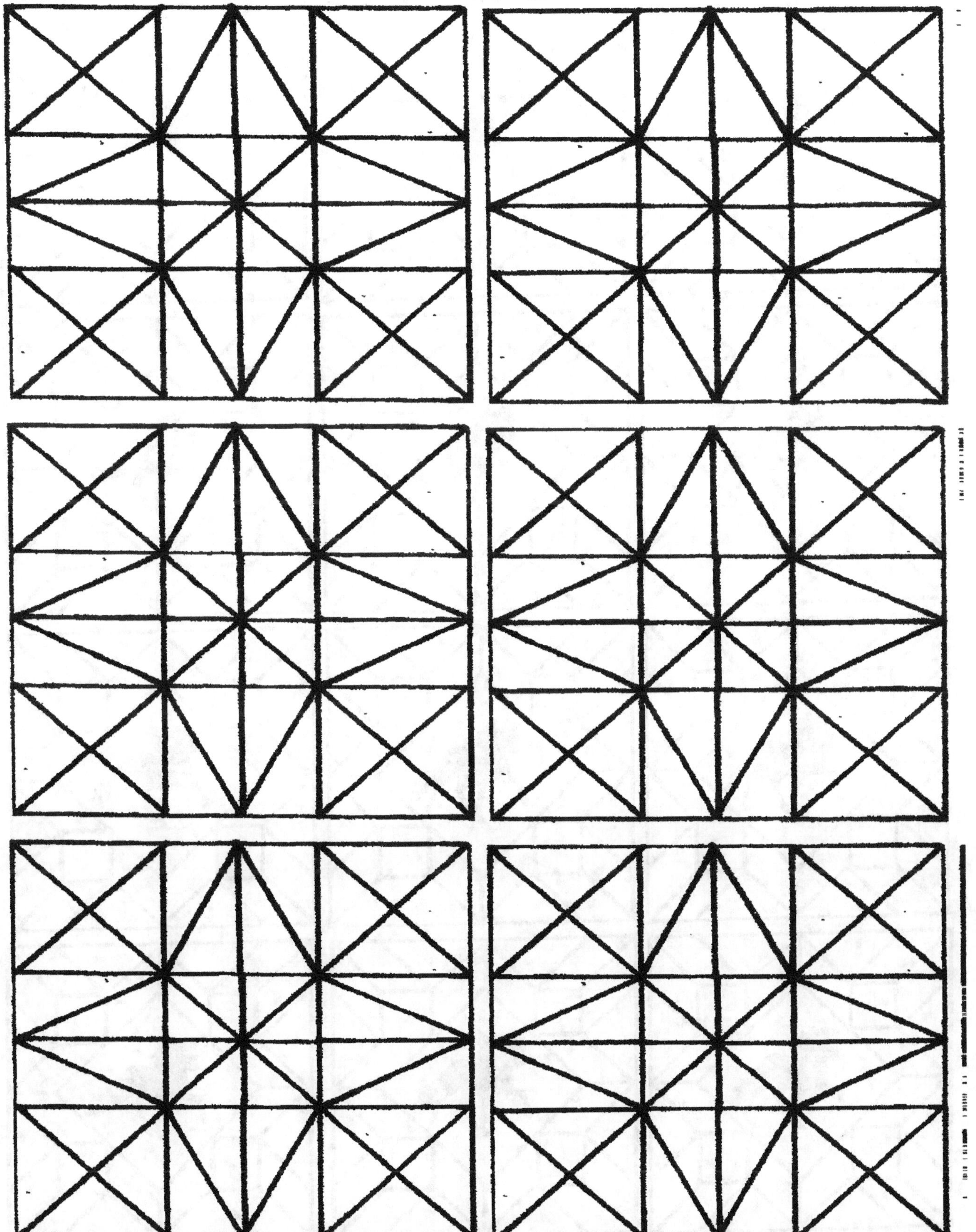

Barn Quilt Peruvian Horse Shawano County Wisconsin

Barn Quilt Liberty Banner Shawano County Wisconsin

Barn Quilt The Red Rooster Shawano County Wisconsin

Barn Quilt Gamma Ray Burst Shawano County Wisconsin

Barn Quilt Barn Raising Shawano County Wisconsin

Barn Quilt Whirlygig Shawano County Wisconsin

Barn Quilt Star Bound Swanano County Wisconsin

Barn Quilt Star of Empire Swanano County Wisconsin

Barn Quilt Wintery Reflection Swanano County Wisconsin

Barn Quilt Twisted Star Swanano County Wisconsin

Barn Quilt Farmer's Pride Swanano County Wisconsin

Barn Quilt Snowy Morning Shawano County Wisconsin

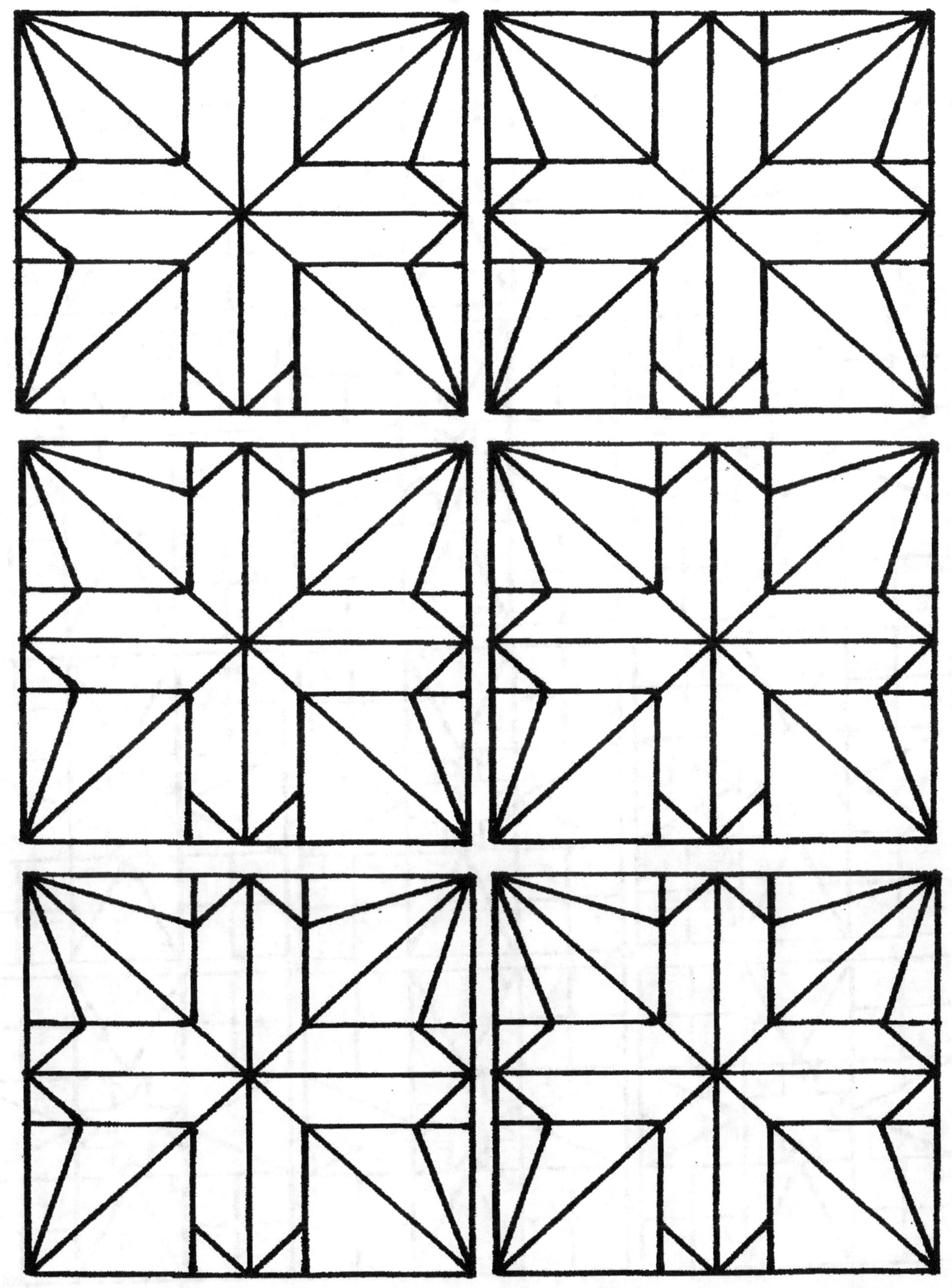

Barn Quilt 54-40 or Fight Shawano County Wisconsin

Barn Quilt Sara's Star Shawano County Wisconsin

Barn Quilt Wisconsin Star County Wisconsin

Barn Quilt Castor & Pollux Shawano County Wisconsin

Barn Quilt Christmas Cactus Central & Northwestern Kansas

Barn Quilt Spools Central & Northwestern Kansas

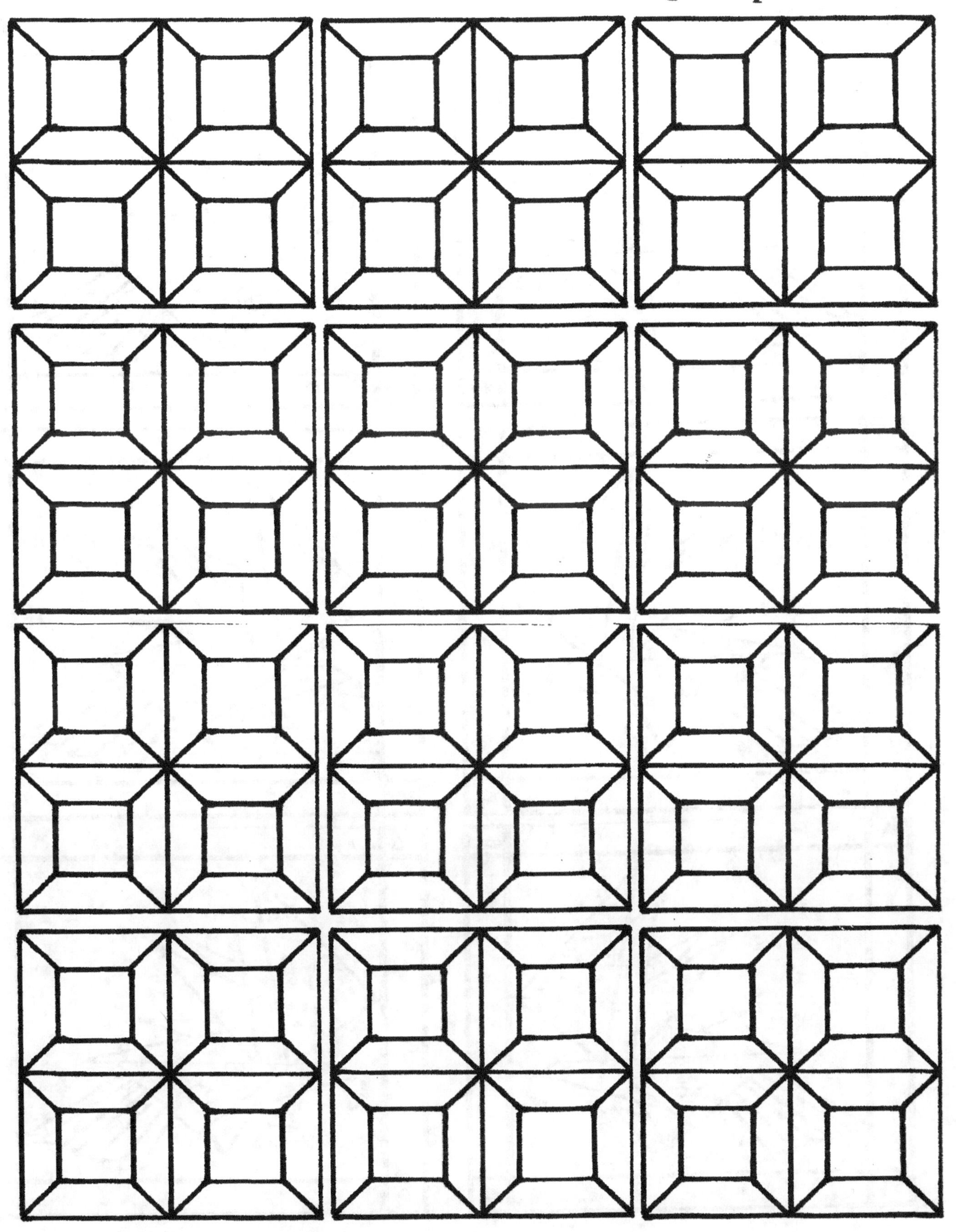

Barn Quilt American Legion Central & Northwestern Kansas

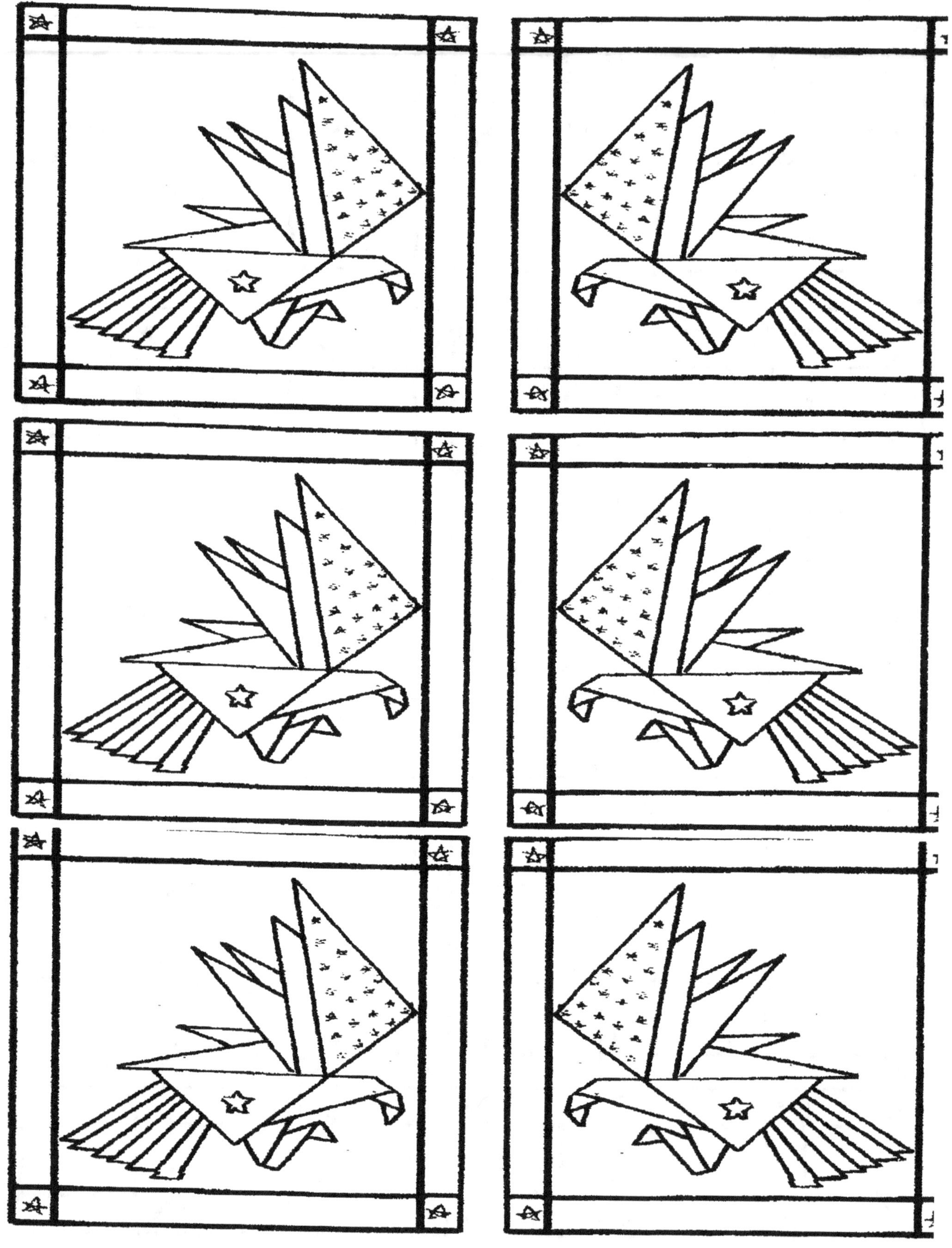

Barn Quilt Stars & Bars Central & Northwestern Kansas

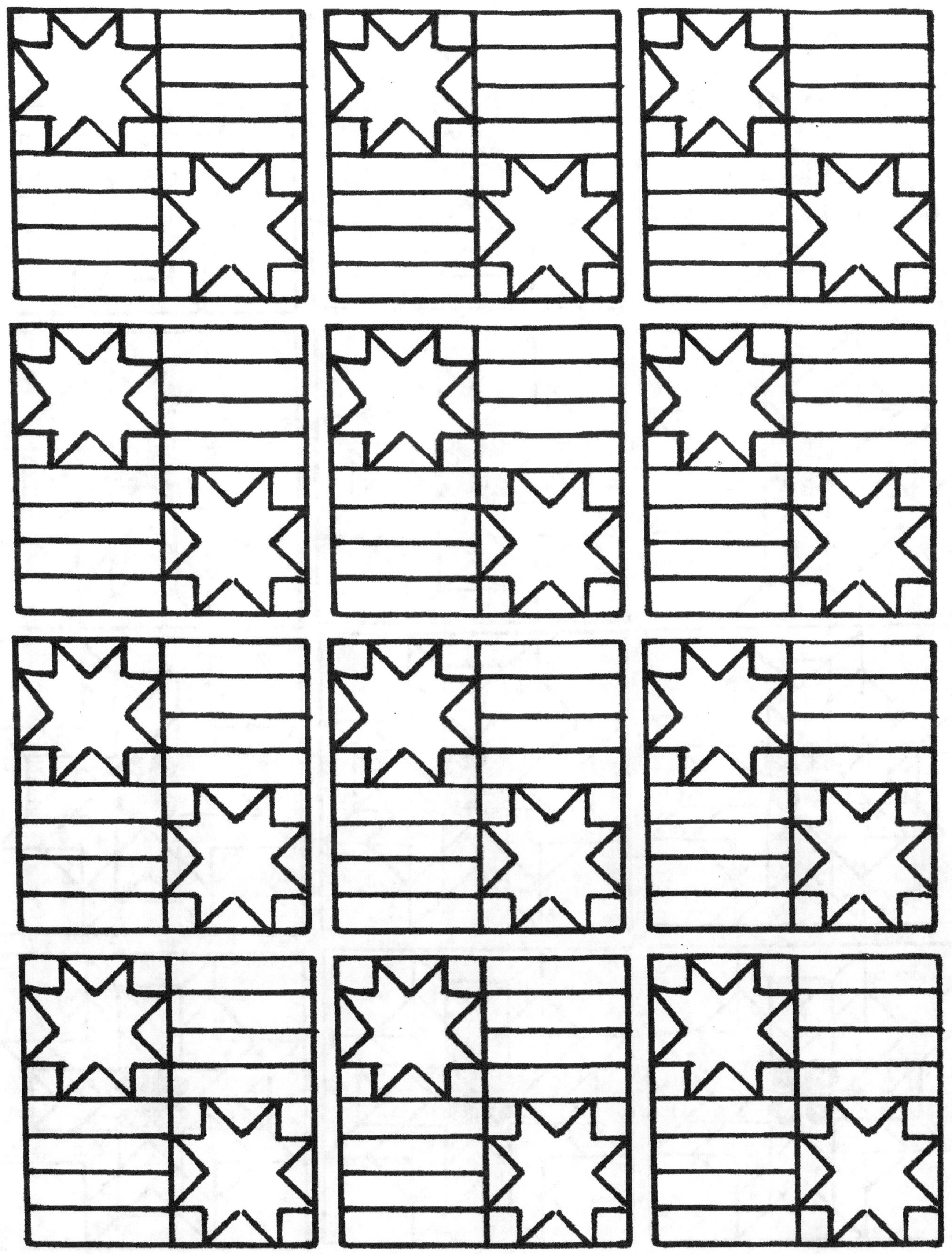

Barn Quilt 4H Star Central & Northwestern Kansas

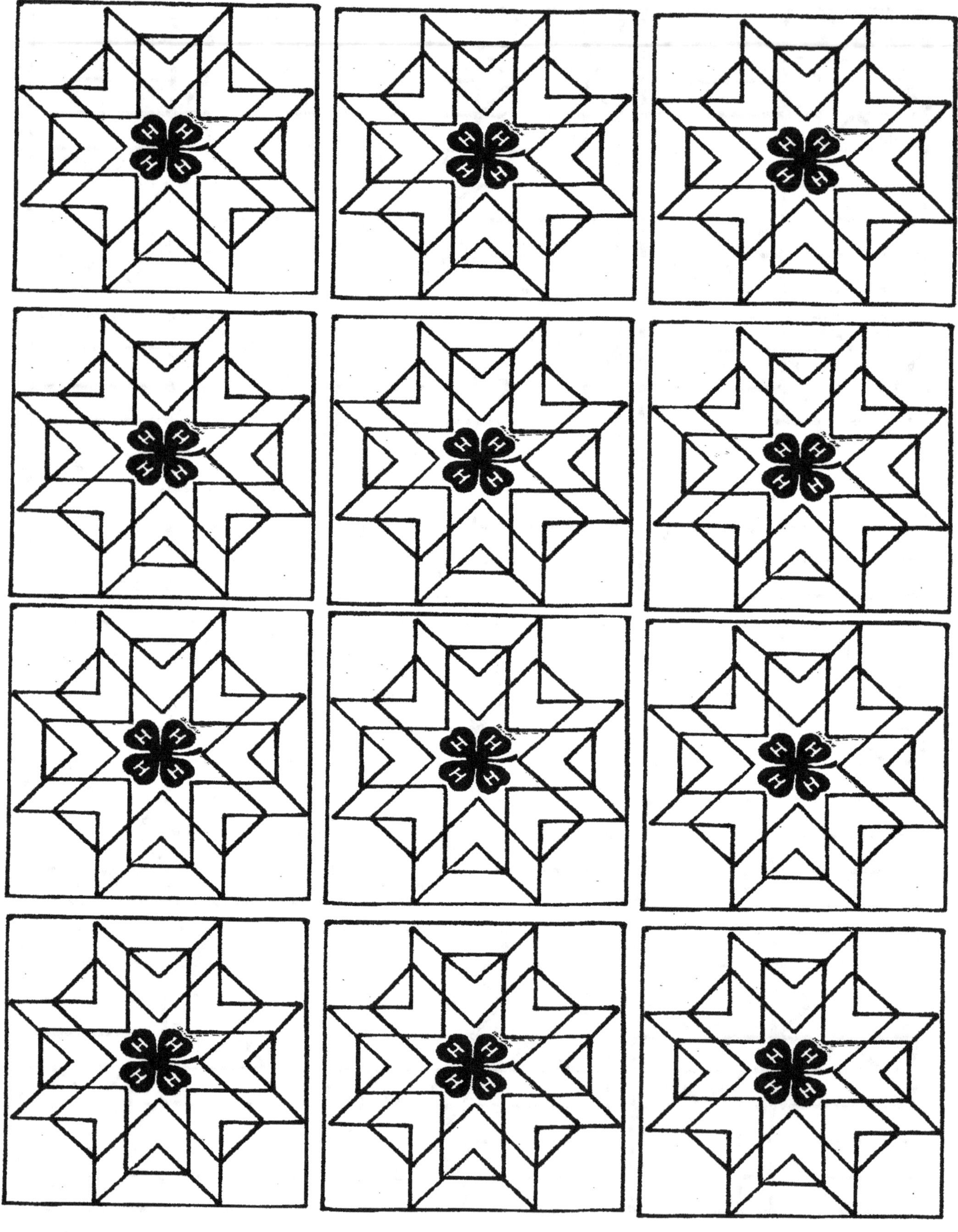

Barn Quilt Patriotic Cross Central & Northwestern Kansas

READING & MATH BOOKS by JOHN H. LETTAU

1st Dimension	Grades 3-6
2nd Dimension	Grades 3-6
Primary Dimension	Grades 1-4
Aztec Math Primary Book One	Grades 1-3
Aztec Math Primary Book Two	Grades 1-3
Aztec Math Intermediate Book One	Grades 3-6
Aztec Math Intermediate Book Two	Grades 3-6
Aztec Math Jr. High Book One	Grades 5-8
Aztec Math Jr. High Book Two	Grades 5-8
Aztec Math Decimal Book	Grades 4-8
Aztec Math Fraction Book	Grades 4-8
Sum-Action Number Puzzle Book One	Grades 3-6
Sum-Action Number Puzzle Book Two	Grades 3-6
Sum-Action Number Puzzle Primary Book One	Grades 1-3
Sum-Action Number Puzzle Primary Book Two	Grades 1-3
Multiplication Number Puzzles	Grades 3-6
Geometric Design Puzzle Book One	Grades 3-6
Geometric Design Puzzle Book Two	Grades 3-6
Aztec Reading Primary Book One	Grades 1-3
Aztec Reading Primary Book Two	Grades 1-3
Math in Action	Grades 3-6
A-Maze-ing Number Puzzles	Grades 3-6
Graph Paper Designs	Grades 2-6
Pick-A-Dilly Papers	Grades 3-6
Awards for All Reasons	Grades 1-6
Time Marches On	Grades 1-3
Pennies, Nickels & Dimes	Grades 1-3
Super-Sum Activity Cards	Grades 3-6
Learning Center Game Boards	Grades 1-3
Aztec Design Coloring Book	Grades 1-6

John Lettau Coloring Books

American Barn Quilt Coloring Books

Shawano County Wisconsin Barn Quilt Coloring Book 1
Shawano County Wisconsin Barn Quilt Coloring Book 2
Shawano County Wisconsin Barn Quilt Coloring Book 3
Green County Wisconsin Barn Quilt Coloring Book
Delaware County Iowa Barn Quilt Coloring Book
Tennessee Appalachain Barn Quilt Coloring Book 1
Tennessee Appalachain Barn Quilt Coloring Book 2
Franklin County Vermont Barn Quilt Coloring Book 1
Franklin County Vermont Barn Quilt Coloring Book 2
Gibson County Indiana Barn Quilt Coloring Book 1
Gibson County Indiana Barn Quilt Coloring Book 2
Lake County California Barn Quilt Coloring Book

Geometric Patterns

Geometric Design Coloring Book 1
Geometric Design Coloring Book 2
Geometric Design Coloring Book 3
Geometric Design Coloring Book 4
Geometric Design Coloring Book 5

Graph Paper Designs

Create your own geometric designs with Graph Paper Designs.

Order...John H. Lettau at Amazon.com